MW00714141

GLENN and His GOAT

Find Grandpa's Gold

Written by
Sue Stuever Battel

Illustrated by Alissa Empsey

Cover design by Robin Fight

Chapter One

Little Glenn sat in the wooden chair with his elbows on the large kitchen table. He peered out the window as his big brother Alfred made his way down the dirt path to the road. He watched as Alfred took each step in his brown boots. Glenn rested his cheek on the palm of his hand as Alfred swung the family axe over his shoulder and stepped out of sight.

Alfred was twelve now, and big, so he had his very own job. The money he earned chopping trees for old Mister Elmer was much needed by the family. Since Grandpa had passed away in the fall, Mother and the children were all alone. Money was hard to come by.

Little Glenn sat up in the chair. He did not want to be little anymore. He was ready to help the family. He was eight years old and strong enough to swing the axe.

"Mother," he asked, "when may I work like Alfred?"

"You remember, my sweet boy," Mother said. "No boots, no work. And we don't have the money for boots for you."

Glenn felt if he could work, he could earn money for boots. If he had boots, he could earn money for the family. He thought about this as Mother moved out of the room. It was time for the two youngest children, Glenn's sisters, to take a nap. Mother looked tired, too.

Chapter Two

Glenn stood up from the chair in the little cabin at the edge of the forest. Mother and the babies would be napping for a bit longer. Alfred was away cutting trees in his brown boots.

Glenn pulled on his green

cap. He pulled open the wooden cabin door and stepped outside. It was cold, and he had no boots to cover his feet, but he made up his mind to take a walk to clear his thinking.

Glenn headed for the old shed. Inside, a tiny goat heard his soft footsteps. The goat let out loud sounds: *Maa-maa*! *Maa-maa*!

"You can come with me," Glenn said to the goat. "Let's go." He opened the gate. The goat hopped next to the boy.

Glenn had only owned the young goat for less than a

year. When the kind man offered him to the family, Mother said, "Thank you, but no." She felt they had no use for a small animal that did not provide food for the family. But as she talked with the man and saw how happy the silly critter made Glenn— running and jumping in the yard, stopping for the boy to catch up, then running and leaping all over again—she agreed. As long as Glenn built a sturdy pen for the goat to live in, he could keep it.

Mother almost changed her mind the very next day. Glenn strode into the kitchen to show Mother the first egg laid by the hens now that the days were getting longer.

"Mother!" he said. "A golden egg!" The egg was brown, not really gold, but to Glenn it was as good as gold.

Glenn left the cabin door wide open. As Mother turned to put the egg in a bowl, an

odd, soft *clip-clop clip-clop clip-clop* grew nearer and nearer.

Sure as the sun rose, the silly new goat had climbed out of its pen and marched into the kitchen. It placed its

front hooves onto Mother's clean kitchen table. Then the goat helped itself to a fresh-baked cornmeal muffin!

"Muffin! Muffin!" Mother shouted. "My muffin! Get that goat out of my kitchen!"

Glenn's mother used corn to grind into meal, and she made the most yummy muffins on the cookstove.

Glenn ran the goat out of the house and set to work making the pen walls higher. From that day forward, the goat had a name: Muffin.

Chapter Three

The leaves crunched under his bare feet as Glenn went into the forest. Muffin, the goat, stayed at his side.

Glenn looked down at the worms coming up from the thawing ground. The snow had melted. Spring was coming.

Glenn was thinking about being rich—about finding a pile of gold and rubies in the forest. As he walked forward, head down toward the muddy ground, he could see the shimmering prize in his mind. Rubies and riches would fix his family's problems. He would be able to buy food and boots! He would pile gold into his little

wagon and—

As Glenn took the next step,

a red squirrel ran right across

his bare toes. Glenn's eyes

chased the squirrel to the

tip-top of a tall tree. He could

just see it climb to the end

of a long branch. The silly

squirrel stretched out to lick

at a little icicle.

As his eyes were now turned upward, Glenn felt the sun warming his cheeks. It had been a long winter without Grandpa. It had seemed as if the cold and sad season would never end.

An opening in the trees above caught Glenn's eyes—a big circle of sky above the dark forest. As the sun reached its peak above him, it filled the circle with a golden light.

The golden sunrays shone on the trees in a way young Glenn had never noticed before.

Now snapped out of his daydream, he noticed the world around him. He saw the sun warming the tree bark. He heard the chittering of the squirrel. His ears picked up the far-off *tap-tap-tap* of a bold woodpecker drumming away at a tree. This part of the forest looked extra beautiful to Glenn.

As he turned round and round, he admired the

golden cast of the sunlight on God's world. He felt strong and warm. He felt hopeful. He felt in his heart that he could help his family.

"Will I find gold?" he found himself asking out loud.

As he spun around, seeing things he had never seen before, he spotted a great bald eagle flying in the sky.

The eagle crossed the patch of open sky from where the golden sun shone. How Glenn loved all of God's critters. Animals made him feel happy. Animals! Where was Muffin?

Chapter Four

As he was the second of four children, Glenn could not wait to be big enough to help the family like his strong older brother. Mother kept busy caring for the two baby sisters. Glenn felt as if Muffin was his best pal. The goat listened and never talked back.

Where was Muffin? His best pal was gone!

"Maa-maa!" shouted Glenn. Sometimes he called for Muffin in the goat's own language. "Maa-maa!" he cried.

Muffin did not answer. Muffin did not come.

Walking back over his steps, Glenn looked for Muffin. He looked left and right. He looked to and fro.

Just then a patch of brown fur behind a great, tall tree caught his eye. "Muffin!"

But Muffin did not come to Glenn. Muffin always came to Glenn.

Glenn drew closer to the tree. "You silly goat!" he said. "Why are you licking the tree?"

Muffin had found a tasty,

damp part of the tree. A branch had broken off above. Something wet ran down the bark. The something wet tasted good to Muffin.

Glenn put a finger to the clear liquid then touched it to his mouth. "Sweet!" he shouted. "A sweet treat for my silly, sweet goat."

Glenn pressed his finger to

the wet stuff again as Muffin
continued to lick away. Sap!

It was the tree's sap flowing
down the bark. It had the
faint, sweet taste of ... of ...

Glenn searched his memory
to recall the familiar taste.
The wind blew a faded
brown leaf across his foot.
Glenn picked up the leaf.
It had fallen in the autumn

and stayed intact under the winter snow. Glenn knew the leaf.

Grandpa had taught Glenn to know the trees, the animals, and much of what grew around their little cabin by name. Like the feathers on a bird helped him know the name of the bird, the leaves told him the name of the tree.

This was the leaf of a sugar maple tree. He knew because it had five main points.

He laid the leaf in the palm of his hand. He could hear Grandpa's voice in his head as he counted. "One, two, three, four, five points on the leaf," he said—the same number as the five fingers on his hand.

This was a sugar maple tree. And this was sugar maple sap! The faint sweet taste? It was the taste of Grandpa's maple syrup!

Muffin was licking maple sap, and the squirrel had licked an icicle at the end of a broken maple twig to get a taste of the same sweet sap.

Glenn looked over the

bark of the sugar maple tree that Muffin had found. The bark had long peeling pieces going up and down the tree. He looked around him for other trees that matched and found another tree with long peeling lines in its bark. And another. And another!

The forest was full of sugar maple trees. "These trees

must be chock full of sap," Glenn said to Muffin as if the goat could understand what it heard, which it could not.

Glenn had found a grove of sugar maple trees. Grandpa

had told him there was "gold" in the forest. Grandpa had promised that when he was able to get out of bed, he would show little Glenn how to get the "gold." But Grandpa never got better. He was never able to get out of bed. And now he had passed away, taking the secret of his gold with him to Heaven.

"There is no time to worry about something as silly as gold," Glenn said to Muffin. Then he turned on his heel and headed out of the forest.

"I am going to surprise Mother. I will show her I am big. I will show her that I can help as much as Alfred does."

Muffin hopped and jumped behind Glenn—the goofy

goat never walked in a line—
as they rushed back toward
the cabin.

Chapter Five

Glenn found just what he was looking for among Grandpa's things.

He gathered them up. Glenn and Muffin made their way back to the forest once again. Glenn set to work using his late grandpa's tools.

He drilled a hole in each sugar maple tree. Round and round went the brace and bit as he drilled the sharp tip through the bark.

He used a small hammer to tap a spile into each hole. The hammer *tap-tap-tapped* against the small metal spouts. As soon as he could insert each spile— *drip-drip-drip*—out came slow, fat drips of sweet sap. Glenn hung metal buckets from each spile. The sap dripped into the buckets.

By the time Glenn finished tapping the last tree, the sap from the first tree had covered the bottom of its bucket. The sap was beautiful and clear.

He thought for a moment. The sap wasn't gold. But it was special. It was sweet. It was "hidden" in the forest. And Glenn would make it into something even sweeter.

Chapter Six

With Muffin at his side, Glenn made another trip back out of the forest and to the cabin. Glenn peeked into a window. He could see that Mother and the babies were starting to stir. To keep the surprise, he led Muffin back into the shed. He helped Mother with supper as if nothing happened during the nap—as if he had not made the find of his life.

He told Mother about the nice walk he and Muffin had taken. He told her about the bold woodpecker and the bald eagle and the red squirrel. But he did not talk about the sap.

The sound of Alfred's boots drew near the cabin. The wooden door opened wide. Alfred was home from a long day's work.

Too excited to wash up first,
Alfred dropped all he had
in his pocket onto the table.
"Look, Mother! Mister Elmer
paid me today," he said.
Alfred dropped a handful of
shiny coins onto the wooden
surface.

Glenn wished he had coins
to give to Mother. He wanted

to help the family, too. He
wanted to make Mother
proud. He wanted to buy
food for his baby sisters. He
wanted to buy his very own
brown boots.

Glenn would do all this and
more. He had a plan.

The next morning after
breakfast, Alfred
strode down the

road to his job in his brown boots. Mother laid down with the babies for a nap. Glenn went outside to get Muffin out of his pen.

Glenn led Muffin up the big hill to the barn. He went inside to search for something. Soon enough he found it. Glenn rolled Grandpa's big iron kettle from the top floor of the big barn. He rolled it down the hill and into the yard.

He went back into the barn to search again. It had been

years since Grandpa kept
horses. Glenn remembered
where the old dusty horse
halters hung in the corner
of the old milk house. Now it
was time for Muffin to help.

Glenn made the old leather
horse halter straps into a
pulling harness for Muffin.
He attached his little wagon.
With some fixing, he had the

goat and wagon ready to go. Into the forest they went— Glenn plodding along in his bare feet and Muffin pulling the wagon.

Once in the forest, Glenn gathered the buckets of clear, sweet sap and loaded them into the wagon. Off he and Muffin went, back to the cabin yard to dump the sap into Grandpa's big black kettle.

Again and again, Glenn and Muffin made the trip until Mother and the babies were ready to wake up from their nap.

Guided by Glenn, Muffin pulled the little wagon full of buckets of sap to the kettle.

Chapter Seven

For the next four days, when Mother laid down for a nap with the babies, right after Alfred and his axe made their way down the road, Glenn and Muffin headed to the forest.

By Friday the kettle was full.

That morning, after breakfast and after Alfred and his boots stepped their way down the road, Glenn had a question. "Mother, may I light a fire in the yard?" Glenn asked.

"Yes, you may," Mother replied with a knowing smile. "Be careful."

Glenn was surprised Mother said yes. He was

more surprised at what she said next. "You can use wood from the pile. Grandpa cut some extra when he was feeling well."

When Mother laid down for her nap with the babies, Glenn gathered kindling, twigs, and logs. He placed them under the kettle full of sap. He started his fire.

Glenn added more and more wood to keep the fire burning strong. The sap in the kettle began to get warm. Steam began to roll off, and the sap began to boil. The sap boiled harder. Big clouds of steam went into the sky from the iron kettle. The sap inside turned darker and darker.

All day long Glenn burned

more and more wood under the kettle. More and more steam rose into the sky.

Glenn missed supper. He was too excited to be hungry.

With a long spoon, Glenn

reached for the sap inside.

It was no longer clear, sweet sap that poured off the spoon. Now it was a thicker, darker, golden liquid. It dripped off the spoon in thick, slow drops.

Glenn had made maple syrup—buckets of it.

Glenn rushed into the cabin to Mother, as fast as he could,

holding a spoonful of syrup.
"You missed din—" Mother
started to say.

Glenn talked fast. "Taste it,
Mother!" Glenn said.

Mother dipped a clean
finger into the pool of syrup
on the big spoon. A rich
golden liquid clung to her
fingertip.

She put the finger to her

lips and smiled. "You found Grandpa's gold," she said to her son proudly.

Glenn was surprised! Mother knew of the gold?

Glenn told Mother all about the sap. He told how Muffin found it. He told how he used Grandpa's tools.

"I'll fetch a jar so you can

bring the 'gold' into the kitchen," Mother told Glenn.

"A jar?" Glenn asked. "I will need lots and lots of jars."

"Lots and lots of jars? How much maple syrup did you make?" asked Mother.

"I made buckets of syrup!" Glenn said.

Mother's eyes grew wide.

Chapter Eight

The next morning, Mother asked Glenn and Alfred to stay home with their baby sisters. Mother would go to town to sell some of the maple syrup. Mother smiled big as she packed her market basket.

Mother caught a ride to town in a friend's horse and buggy. Glenn helped her load the casks of maple syrup into the buggy. Mother's face smiled brightly.

Glenn and Alfred cared for their sisters all day. They fed them the soup Mother left behind. It was made from the last of the food

from the garden.
Most times
Mother would
worry about
running
out of food.
This morning
she had sung
while she
made the
soup.

Mother even left behind fresh cornmeal muffins. She had told the children not to eat the muffins until she came back home. The children looked at the muffins all day, but they did not touch them.

As the sun began to set, the children heard the horse's hooves on the road. They met Mother in the yard. She would not let them see what was in her market basket. She told the children to go inside the cabin first.

Inside the cabin, Mother's market basket was full to the top. She told Glenn to turn around and cover his eyes. She placed the basket under the table.

"Turn around, Son," Mother said. "You may look."

One by one, Mother pulled out items she was able to buy with the money from the maple syrup: cloth to make new dresses for her and the babies, a new axe head for Alfred, a huge sack of flour, and one more thing—a pair of brown boots for Glenn!

Glenn couldn't wait to try on his new boots! "Wait," Mother said. "We must do one thing first."

Mother served the cornmeal muffins. Alfred began to take a bite. "Wait," she said. "Glenn, go get your goat."

Glenn led Muffin into the kitchen. Mother poured the liquid gold over a cornmeal muffin for Glenn. She poured syrup over a muffin for Alfred and the girls.

This time she gave Muffin his very own muffin, too.

MORE SILVER TALES FROM THE GOOD AND THE BEAUTIFUL LIBRARY

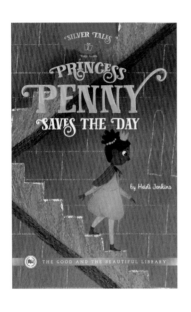

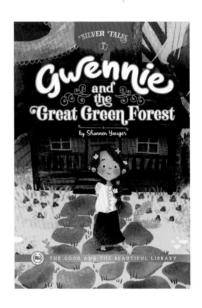

Princess Penny Saves the Day

By Heidi Jenkins

Gwennie and the Great Green Forest

By Shannen Yauger